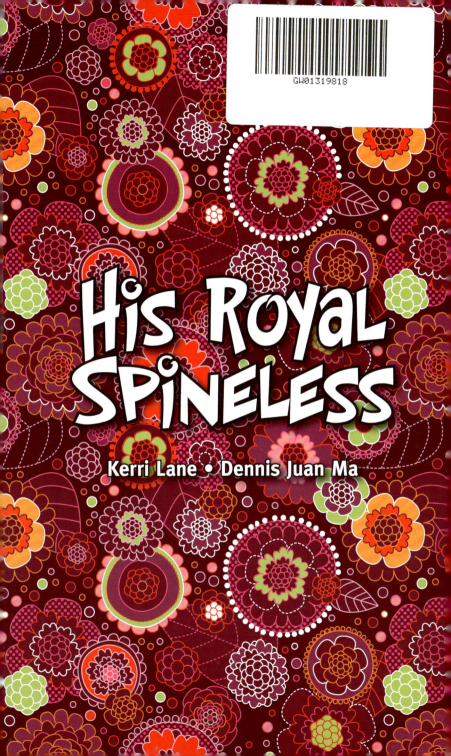

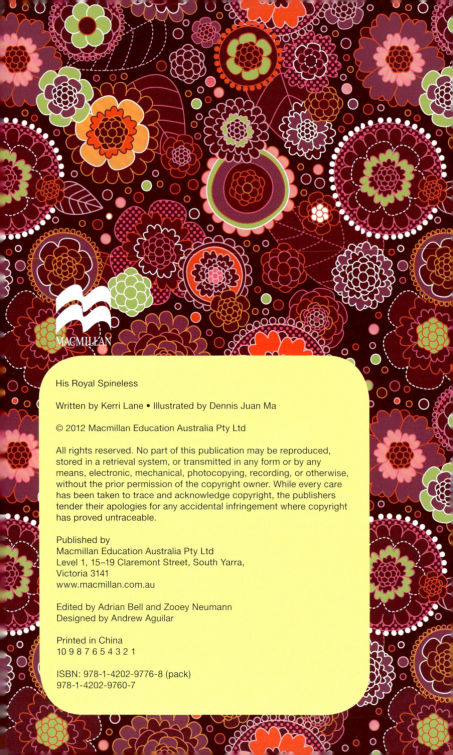

His Royal Spineless

Written by Kerri Lane • Illustrated by Dennis Juan Ma

© 2012 Macmillan Education Australia Pty Ltd

All rights reserved. No part of this publication may be reproduced, stored in a retrieval system, or transmitted in any form or by any means, electronic, mechanical, photocopying, recording, or otherwise, without the prior permission of the copyright owner. While every care has been taken to trace and acknowledge copyright, the publishers tender their apologies for any accidental infringement where copyright has proved untraceable.

Published by
Macmillan Education Australia Pty Ltd
Level 1, 15–19 Claremont Street, South Yarra,
Victoria 3141
www.macmillan.com.au

Edited by Adrian Bell and Zooey Neumann
Designed by Andrew Aguilar

Printed in China
10 9 8 7 6 5 4 3 2 1

ISBN: 978-1-4202-9776-8 (pack)
978-1-4202-9760-7

Contents

1 Cauliflower Ears 7

2 Under Attack 11

3 Run for Your Life! 19

4 Lions? 25

5 The Happy Prince 33

Author 38

Illustrator 39

Read More Sprints 40

Characters

My peaceful lifestyle is being ruined! And where are the sandwiches?

Why does this always happen to us? We have to do something to make it STOP!

King Ron

Queen Petula

Chapter 1

Cauliflower Ears

King Ron lifted his earmuffs. "Has that **noise** stopped yet?" he asked.

Queen Petula opened the visor of her helmet. "What did you say?" she `yelled`.

Everyone in the castle was at their wits' end. Ever since the king's cousin, Prince Cedric, had arrived, all they heard was **SCREAMING**. And **crying**. And **sobbing**.

They couldn't talk. They couldn't think. They couldn't watch CWW (that's Castle Wide Wrestling). All because they couldn't hear anything but Cedric! They had even given him a nickname, "His Royal Spineless."

"How can a great big prince like him be so **SCARED** of everything!" complained Princess Daisy. She had pieces of cauliflower over her ears.

"Quick!" said the queen. "Hide! Here he comes again!"

The royal family had barely taken two steps when the door to the great hall was thrown back and the prince ran **SCREAMING** into the room.

"Help me! Help me!" he cried. He was quite tall and very, very **skinny**. In fact, he looked a lot like a four-legged spider, a spider wearing a wonky gold crown that **jiggled** on the top of his head.

"It's after me!" Prince Cedric shrieked. "It'll **ATTACK** us all!"

Chapter 2

UNDER ATTACK

The king looked at the screaming prince nervously. He couldn't see anything dangerous, but he wasn't taking any chances. "**ATTACK**? Really?" he said. "Then summon the…er… watch-am-a-call-its. The em… **fighting** people!"

The queen sighed. "Do you mean your **army**, dear?" she said.

Within an hour, the royal **army** was camped outside the castle, prepared to defend it from its enemies.

Back in the great hall, King Ron tapped his foot impatiently and **glared** at Prince Cedric. "Well?" he said. "Where's this thing that's going to **ATTACK** us?"

"It was right behind me," said the prince. "It was **awful**. A terrible, black shape, like a giant, four-legged spider."

"That's your **Shadow**!" exclaimed Princess Poppy. Prince Cedric paused in mid-squeal.

"What? That's ridiculous," he said. "Who's afraid of their own **Shadow**?"

"You!" shouted everyone in the great hall.

"**Disgrace** the army!" boomed the king.

The queen sighed again. "I think you mean '**dismiss**' the army, dear," she said.

"Oh, yes," said the king. "And bring sandwiches! With every kind of filling. Except fish paste. Yuck!"

When Cedric was handed a plate, his eyes nearly **popped**. His face went very pale. "That's not…cheese? Is it?" he whimpered. "Yeargh!" Suddenly, the plate went flying and so did Cedric, right under the table!

Princess Poppy peeked under the table. "Cheese?" she said. "You're afraid of cheese?" She shook her head at him and clicked her tongue loudly. At the sound of the clicking tongue, Prince Cedric screeched in **terror**. He ran for the door, tipping the table over as he went.

Princess Daisy **yelped** as a pickle whacked her on the nose. Princess Poppy picked lettuce out of her hair. The queen wiped egg off her face. The king scrambled around on the floor, looking for his favourite lamb-and-jam sandwiches. "**Mine! Mine! Mine!**" he cried as he dived at each one.

They weren't free of Cedric for long. Faster than lightning, he came speeding back through the great hall. His skinny knees were almost hitting his chest as he ran. "Mouse! Mouse!" he cried.

As she watched him fly past, Princess Daisy covered her ears. "Let's hope the **mouse** chases him all the way back to his own castle!" she said.

No sooner had she spoken than Cedric was back. He was moving so fast they almost didn't see him. But they heard him! "Lady with a beard! Lady with a beard!" he **howled**.

"Do we have a lady with a beard in the castle?" the queen frowned.

"Only that painting of your mother, my dear," the king answered.

"He's afraid of paintings of grannies, too?" gasped Princess Poppy.

It was time for a **family meeting**.

Chapter 3

Run For Your Life!

"Right," said the king. "Who are we declaring **WAR** on today?"

"No one," said the queen. "We…"

"The **dungeon**, then?" interrupted the king. "Are we throwing someone in the **dungeon**?"

"It's Cedric!" said the queen crossly.

"Cedric is going in the **dungeon**?" said the king. "Good idea!"

"No!" Princess Daisy yelled. "We just want him to stop being afraid of everything so we can get some **peace**."

"I might have the answer," said the queen. "Dr Bill, the royal psychiatrist, says that if we find something Cedric **loves**, he'll focus on that and forget to be **scared**."

"But he hates everything!" said Princess Poppy. "How can we find something he **loves**?"

"That's certainly going to be our challenge," the queen answered.

And it was. For the next five days, they tried showing Cedric flowers, fairies, and fungus. They tried playing tennis, twister, and tiddlywinks. They read him stories about porcupines, piglets, and pandas. But everything they tried made Cedric howl in **terror**. The noise was **unbearable**!

The royal doctor was run off his feet. He fixed sore ears here and sore heads there. In the end, he put himself to bed with a headache!

The king was so upset, he could hardly eat. His daily diet of about 50 lamb-and-jam sandwiches dropped to a mere 40!

"We just have to think *harder*!" said Queen Petula. "What could Cedric like?"

Princess Daisy thought the **cowardly** prince might like a puppy. There was nothing scary about puppies. Unless you were Cedric! He took one look at the cute little mutt, screeched louder than ever before, and ran. The puppy, delighted by this wonderful game, **chased** the prince, who ran even faster.

He **ran** through the great hall, into the throne room, across the moat, back over the moat, into the royal sandwich kitchen, through the royal pizza parlour, and back into the great hall. Then, he did it all over again. And again!

He ran so fast that by the time he was finished, his feet had **pounded** a trench in the stone floor. It came up to his waist, but still he ran!

Chapter 4

Lions?

Everybody was talking about the trench. Except Mavis, the royal cook! She'd been so busy baking 50 **pies** for dinner that she hadn't heard about the trench. This was why she ended up with **pie** on her face, and in her hair, and her nose, and her eyes. And it was also why she had **steam** coming out of her ears when she climbed out of the trench.

It was also why everyone in the palace had sandwiches AGAIN that night, and why they were all **grumbling**. Except for the king. He loved sandwiches! But only with lamb and jam. He checked carefully to make sure Mavis wasn't trying to give him fish paste.

"This is a **disaster**!" wailed Poppy. "We have to think of something. What about the Colympics? Everyone loves the Castle Olympics, and Cedric is very good at **running**."

It was a **BRILLIANT** idea. They thought it would solve all their problems. Alas, it didn't work out like that. First, Cedric was scared of the running shoes. Then, he was terrified when he heard he would have to stand next to a line. "No, Cedric," Princess Poppy tried to explain, "lines, not lions. The lines won't **ROAR** at you, I promise!"

Even after Cedric finally agreed to stand by the line, it still went wrong. As soon as the **STARTING CANNON** went off, Cedric ran screaming. As usual. This time, though, he didn't stop! He ran off the racetrack, out through the castle gate, and into the deep, dark *forest*.

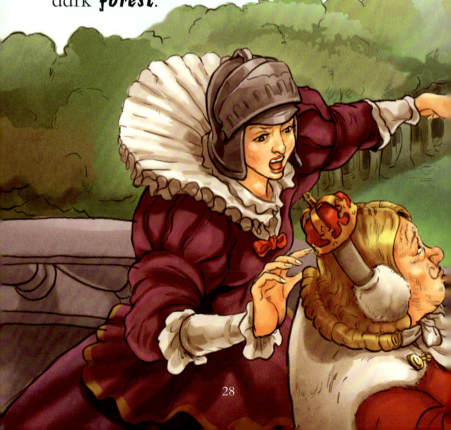

"Oh, no!" exclaimed the queen. "Can you imagine how terrified he'll be, alone in the forest with all those wild **beasts**? We have to go and find him."

The king summoned the royal **army** and led his soldiers into the forest. They finally found Prince Cedric, but it took all night. He kept **hiding** because he was scared of the horses.

"Do we have to take him home?" pleaded the king. He'd eaten all his sandwiches, and he always got **grumpy** when the food ran out.

"You're not being any help at all!" the queen scolded.

"I am!" protested King Ron. "I tried to find something he'd like. I gave him some **worms**. I quite like worms. I had them on toast once."

Princess Daisy sighed. "That was spaghetti, Father," she said.

"There must be something he likes," said the queen **DESPERATELY**.

For two more days, they tried everything. Poppy tried strawberries, but the thought of them brought Cedric out in **hives**. Daisy offered coloured pencils, but the pointy ends sent him running away **SCREAMING**. The queen gave him a board game, but the dots on the dice **terrified** him. Mavis cooked him spinach pie, but it turned out he was scared **stiff** of the colour green. The king came up with the idea of a swarm of angry bees, which sent everyone in the castle **running**.

Then, finally, one day, everyone awoke to silence…

Chapter 5

The Happy Prince

"What did you do?" King Ron asked the queen.

"I finally found something he likes!" she replied. "He's stopped thinking about all the scary things and is only thinking about the thing he **loves**!"

The king laughed and clapped. "**Celebration** time," he said. "Bring sandwiches. Lots of them!"

Mavis looked nervous as she put the huge platter of sandwiches down on the table. The king grabbed one and took a bite. And **spat** it out!

"Fish paste!" he gasped. He quickly searched through the piles of sandwiches. "These are all fish paste! Where's my lamb and jam?"

He looked up in **shock** as Princess Daisy and Princess Poppy led Cedric, blindfolded, into the great hall. They brought him up to the platter of sandwiches and removed the blindfold. When he saw the fish paste treats, Cedric's eyes **lit up**.

"This?" gasped the king. "This is the only thing he's not scared of? **Disgusting** fish paste? Never! I won't have it! Take these sandwiches away!"

But as soon as the servants carried the platter out of the hall, Cedric began to **SHRIEK** in fear.

"Please, Father," begged Daisy. "This is the only thing that will shut him up. We need those sandwiches."

As soon as the sandwiches were brought back, Cedric calmed down. He took a sandwich and munched happily. Everyone sighed in **relief**.

"At last!" said the queen. "Problem solved. We just have to make sure that the castle is full of fish paste."

King Ron's eyes widened. He threw his hands in the air. With one last look at the fish paste sandwiches, he ran **SCREAMING** from the room.

Cedric looked on curiously. "What is the matter with that man?" he said. "What a **ridiculous** way to carry on."

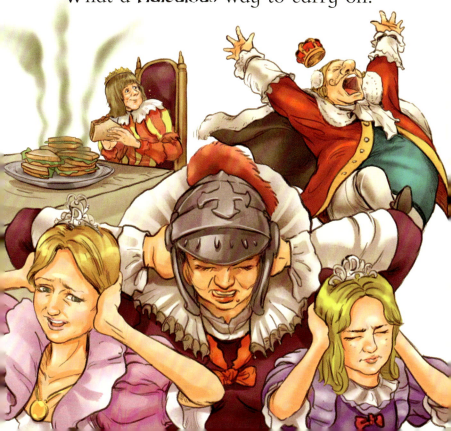

AUTHOR

Kerri Lane is married with four grown-up children and a dog named Bella. She lives and writes at Lake Macquarie, New South Wales. Kerri has written more than 60 children´s books. She always wanted to be a writer. Wait! She also wanted to be tall.

Her dream would be to be a tall writer. So, if you have a stretching rack at home, give her a call. Now´s good. She´s waiting by the phone...

Illustrator

Dennis Juan Ma loves drawing, and it has always been his favourite hobby. He has dreamed of illustrating books since childhood, and now this dream has come true. He has illustrated more than ten books, but he has an appetite for more.

Dennis works and lives in the beautiful city of Auckland, New Zealand. If you ever want to stop him hiking in the mountains or swimming in the sea, just give him a book to illustrate.